10/03

Martin Van Buren

Martin Van Buren

Lesli J. Favor

AMERICA'S
8TH
PRESIDENT

Children's Press®
A Division of Scholastic Inc.
New York / Toronto / London / Auckland / Sydney
Mexico City / New Delhi / Hong Kong
Danbury, Connecticut

Library of Congress Cataloging-in-Publication Data

Favor, Lesli J.
      Martin Van Buren / by Lesli J. Favor.
        p. cm. – (Encyclopedia of presidents)
      Summary: Examines the life of the lawyer politician who became the
eighth president of the United States and led the country through its first serious
depression.
Includes bibliographical references and index.
   ISBN 0-516-22770-X
    1. Van Buren, Martin, 1782–1862—Juvenile literature. 2. Presidents—United
States—Biography—Juvenile literature. [1. Van Buren, Martin, 1782–1862. 2.
Presidents.] I. Title. II. Series.
E387 .F38 2003
973.5'7'092—dc21   2002008778

CHILDREN'S PRESS and associated logos are trademarks and or registered
trademarks of Scholastic Library Publishing. SCHOLASTIC and associated
logos are trademarks and or registered trademarks of Scholastic Inc.
1 2 3 4 5 6 7 8 9 10 R 12 11 10 09 08 07 06 05 04 03

Contents

Chapter 1

Born Under the American Flag

Little Mat

Martin Van Buren was born on December 5, 1782, more than six years after the Declaration of Independence was signed, and a little more than a year after the British army surrendered at Yorktown, Virginia, in the last major battle of the Revolutionary War. When he was elected president 54 years later, Van Buren began a new era for the presidency. He was the first president born after the Declaration of Independence and the Revolutionary War. He was the first president born as a citizen of the new United States and the first whose family was not descended from British ancestors. Van Buren's family descended from Dutch immigrants who arrived in North America in the 1600s.

Martin was born in Kinderhook, New York, a small town near the eastern bank of the Hudson River. *Kinderhook* is Dutch for

Martin Van Buren was born in this simple house in Kinderhook, a village in New York's Hudson Valley.

"children's corner." Like many families in the town, the Van Burens spoke Dutch at home, but also learned English. Little Mat's mother, Maria, was a widow with three children when she married Abraham Van Buren. Together, they had three daughters and three sons.

As Little Mat grew, he worked with his sisters and brothers on the family's farm. The Van Burens had owned and farmed this land for 150 years. The family also used part of their home as a tavern. It sat near the Albany Post Road, the main land route between Albany, 20 miles (32 km) to the north, and New York City, nearly 100 (160 km) miles to the south. The tavern was a rest stop for stagecoaches traveling along the road. There travelers and drivers could rest and buy food and drink.

The Tavern and Politics

When Martin was not delivering farm produce for his father, he listened to travelers talk in the tavern. Because Albany was the capital of New York State, many of the travelers were lawyers, politicians, and businessmen. They discussed current events and politics, sometimes debating about how the state and the country should be governed.

Martin learned that people often disagreed about politics. Federalists believed that the national government should be strong and provide help to merchants and businessmen. Anti-Federalists (members of the Democratic-Republican party) thought that state and local governments should hold most of the power. They wanted these local and regional governments to help farmers. Martin's father supported the Anti-Federalists, but he did not argue with Federalists in the tavern. As a businessman, he welcomed customers of all political beliefs. Martin may have learned from his father that a person could have strong beliefs but did not have to argue about them with others.

Over the years, many powerful men stopped at the tavern. Alexander Hamilton was a New York lawyer who had served heroically in the American Revolution. He attended the Constitutional Convention and worked tirelessly to get the Constitution ratified (approved) by New York State. He served as the first secretary of the treasury during the presidency of George Washington and

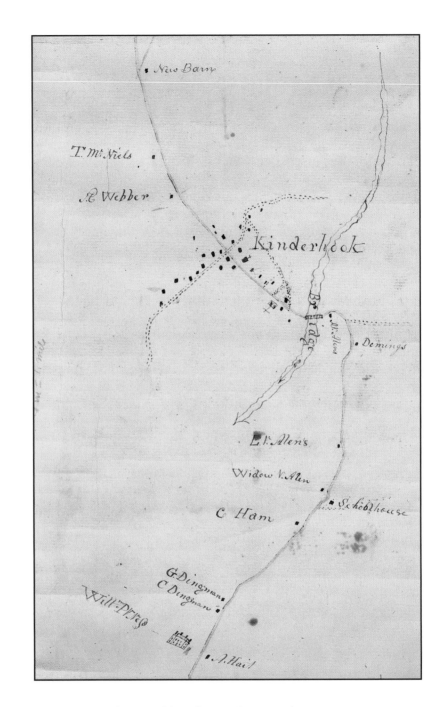

Kinderhook was on the post road from Albany south to New York City.

was a founder of the Federalist party. Another Federalist leader, John Jay, also visited Kinderhook. He served as the first chief justice of the U.S. Supreme Court and negotiated an important treaty with Great Britain. When Martin was twelve, Jay became governor of New York, an office that Martin would one day hold himself.

Among the Anti-Federalists to visit the Van Buren tavern was Aaron Burr, a political enemy of Hamilton's. In 1789, when Martin was six, Burr was elected U.S. senator from New York. He became a powerful political leader in New York, and in 1801 he was elected vice president of the United States.

At election time, Martin got to see visitors from Albany and New York who came to campaign for their candidates. On election day, the tavern was a

Relation to the Roosevelts

Theodore Roosevelt, the 26th president of the United States (1901–1909), and Franklin Roosevelt, the 32nd president (1933–1945), were distant cousins of Martin Van Buren. The Roosevelt family was also descended from early Dutch immigrants to North America.

E.Gridley Sc.

A.BURR, ESQ.

Aaron Burr, a power in New York politics, was a visitor to the Van Buren tavern when Martin was a boy.

polling place, where votes were cast and counted. Martin got to see firsthand how elections worked.

These wealthy lawyers wore fashionable clothes that Martin was not used to seeing. Their coats were richly dyed, and their breeches were velvet. Their heads were topped with white-powdered wigs and stylish hats. Silk stockings and shoes with silver buckles finished out the outfits. These smartly dressed lawyers provided Martin a fascinating glimpse into the habits of the wealthy. Later, when he became a successful political leader, Martin himself would learn to dress elegantly.

Slavery in Kinderhook

When Martin was growing up, slavery was legal in many states, including New York. People in New York's Hudson Valley owned slaves. Martin's father kept six slaves, who worked on the family farm and in the kitchen. Slavery was not made illegal in New York until 1827.

Years later, the question of slavery became one of the most important in politics. During most of his career in politics, Van Buren held to the opinion that each state had the right to allow or forbid slavery. Late in his life, however, his opinions began to shift, and in 1848, he ran for president as an opponent of extending slavery.

Martin's Education

Much of Martin's time was taken up with work on the farm and in the tavern. When he could get away, he attended Kinderhook's one-room schoolhouse. The room was poorly furnished and dim. It was hardly an inviting atmosphere to a young boy. Still, he learned to read and write and proved to be a good student. Later, his father sent him to a nearby secondary school and allowed him to continue there until he was 14. There he learned a little Latin, which was then an important school subject. Martin earned praise from teachers for his achievements, but he always felt that he had a limited education. Even when he was president, he was shy about his skills in writing and speaking!

After leaving school, Martin found a job in a lawyer's office. There were no schools of law in those days. A young man who wanted to become a lawyer could pay an experienced lawyer to "read law" with him, or he could find work in a lawyer's office as an apprentice. Martin and his family could not afford to pay for further study, so Martin went to work. For a small wage, he was expected to sweep floors, tend the fire, run errands, and copy legal papers by hand (there were no copying machines). When his work was done, he could study law books in the office on his own.

Martin worked as apprentice to Francis Silvester, a lawyer in Kinderhook. Like many lawyers, Silvester was also interested in politics. He was a Federalist, favoring a strong national government and government help for merchants and businessmen. Martin, like his father, was a Democratic-Republican who favored more local control and more attention to the needs of small farmers. Martin knew that he and Silvester had different political beliefs, but he kept his politics separate from his work and worked hard to earn Silvester's approval.

Francis Silvester's father was a New York State senator—a member of the state legislature in Albany, which made laws for the state. While Martin was working for his son, Senator Silvester ran for reelection on the Federalist ticket and won. Martin was invited to come to the celebration party, but he would not join in the festivities. He felt he could not celebrate a Federalist victory. Later, Francis Silvester's brother Cornelius tried to persuade Martin to adopt Federalist beliefs, but he could not get Martin to change his mind. Martin worked for Francis Silvester for five years, but he never did change his political views.

During his years as an apprentice, Martin became friends with another family in Kinderhook, the Van Nesses. John P. Van Ness was leader of the Democratic-Republican party in Kinderhook. In 1802, Van Ness ran for a seat in the U.S. House of Representatives, and Martin worked on his campaign. He helped Van Ness win the election.

In gratitude for Martin's hard work on his campaign, Van Ness loaned him money to prepare seriously for a career as a lawyer. Martin moved to New York

City to work for the law firm of John's brother, William Van Ness. Here he had time to study hard for the examination to qualify as a lawyer. In 1803, Martin passed the test and was licensed to practice law in New York State. He went back to Kinderhook and set up his own law office. He was 20 years old.

Chapter 2

Practicing Law —————————————

In 1804, a long dispute between two of the most powerful political leaders in New York ended in tragedy. Aaron Burr was then vice president of the United States under President Jefferson but knew he would not be nominated to run for reelection. He announced plans to run for governor of New York and gained the support of many Federalists. However, the most powerful Federalist in New York, Alexander Hamilton, did not like or trust Burr. He wrote that Burr was "a man of irregular and unsatiable ambition . . . who ought not to be trusted with the reins of government." Burr lost the election and blamed his defeat on Hamilton. He challenged Hamilton to a duel—a personal fight with pistols.

Dueling was illegal in many states, yet Hamilton felt he could not refuse the challenge. So on July 11, 1804, the two men and their two assistants, or "seconds," met at an isolated spot in Weehawken, New Jersey, just across the Hudson River from New York City. Standing 20 paces apart, they waited for one of the seconds to shout "Fire!" When the order came, they fired. Burr's shot hit Hamilton, who died the next day of his wound.

Hamilton's second in the fatal duel was William Van Ness, Martin Van Buren's former boss in Kinderhook. Even though the duel took place in New Jersey, New York officials brought charges against Van Ness for participating in a duel. He asked young Martin Van Buren to defend him in court. (Charges were also brought against Aaron Burr, but he fled the state.)

Martin worked hard on the defense of Van Ness, gaining the support of important leaders in the state, including the Democratic-Republican governor. Van Ness was not convicted of a crime and was released. Martin gained a reputation as a skilled lawyer.

Van Buren had finally outgrown his childhood name, Little Mat. Yet at five feet six inches tall, he would always inspire people to attach "Little" to the nicknames they gave him. As an adult he was sometimes called "Little Van." He was an elegant and tasteful dresser. With his sandy curls, high forehead, and deep-set blue eyes, he cut a fine figure indeed.

Alexander Hamilton is shot in a duel with Aaron Burr in 1804. Hamilton later died of his wounds.

Van Buren returned to Kinderhook, where he took cases from rich and poor alike. Sometimes he defended farmers and small shopkeepers against wealthy landowners and landlords. At other times, he defended landowners. In some of these cases, he helped evict poor tenants from the land of the wealthy.

Many of Van Buren's court cases took him to the Supreme Court in Albany, the state capital, only 20 miles (32 km) from Kinderhook. There he got to know government leaders, forming friendships and contacts that would help him in his own political career. With his cheerful personality and charm, he was a welcome guest at parties and receptions.

With a growing legal practice, Martin was ready to support his own family. On February 21, 1807, he married Hannah Hoes, a young woman from Kinderhook whom he had known since childhood. He was 24 years old, and Hannah three months younger.

Legislator

In 1807, Martin helped his friend Daniel Tompkins get elected governor of New York. In return, Governor Tompkins appointed Martin to the job of surrogate of Columbia County. A surrogate is a type of judge. Martin settled disputes over land and property rights.

Hannah Hoes Van Buren

Hannah Hoes was distantly related to Martin's mother's side of the family. Like Martin, Hannah grew up speaking Dutch. She spoke English with a distinct Dutch accent. Martin affectionately called her "Jannetje," which is Dutch for Hannah.

Hannah was born March 8, 1783, in Kinderhook. After her marriage she gave birth to four sons: Abraham (1807), John (1810), Martin Jr. (1812), and Smith (1817). After the Van Burens moved to Hudson, New York, in 1812, Hannah joined the Presbyterian Church since there was no Dutch Reformed church there. She devoted much of her time to helping the poor. It was said that none but the poor knew her as well as her family. She continued her church work after the family moved to Albany in 1816.

Hannah Hoes married Martin Van Buren in 1807. She gave birth to five sons (one died in infancy), then died of tuberculosis in 1819 at the age of 35.

Then Hannah developed tuberculosis. After a long illness, she died on February 5, 1819, leaving Martin and four young sons. She was buried in the Van Buren plot of the cemetery in Kinderhook. Martin never remarried.

☆☆☆

The post of surrogate was Van Buren's first job in public service. He could use his training as a lawyer, but he could also prepare for a political career. He had helped other men win political positions, and looked forward to gaining an elective office himself. In 1809, he was appointed chairman of the Democratic-Republican meetings in Albany. He became closely acquainted with leaders of the political party.

In 1812, he ran for a seat in the New York State senate. His opponent was the Federalist Edward P. Livingston, a member of one of the most powerful families in the state. The race was close, but Martin had the support he needed to win. In 1813, he took his seat in the state senate and moved his family to the state capital at Albany.

Van Buren had barely taken office when the U.S. Congress declared war on Great Britain. Van Buren supported the War of 1812 and used his position in the state senate to help carry it on. He wrote papers defending the American position and supplied them to other politicians. He helped pass laws to defend New York and the United States against British attack. In 1814, he wrote a *bill* (a proposal for a law) calling on the New York militia to call out 12,000 men for the war effort. The bill passed and became law. New York militiamen helped defend the state's borders against British troops who hoped to invade from Canada.

When Van Buren moved to Albany, it was a small but important city on the Hudson River. Settled by the Dutch in the 1600s, Albany still had many buildings in the Dutch style.

Fast Facts

THE WAR OF 1812

Who: The United States against Great Britain.

When: The U.S. declared war in June 1812. The war was ended by the Treaty of Ghent, signed in December 1814, but fighting continued into January 1815.

Why: Britain was restricting U.S. shipping, seizing cargoes and sailors from U.S. ships. It was also interfering with settlement in U.S. western territories and providing help to Native Americans who were attacking American settlers.

Where: In the United States, Canada, and on the Atlantic Ocean. The U.S. organized several unsuccessful invasions of Canada and lost forts in the Northwest. In 1813, the U.S. Navy defeated a British fleet in Lake Erie, leading to land victories at Detroit and at the Thames River (in nearby Ontario). In 1814, the British captured Washington, D.C., and burned public buildings, but were defeated soon afterward in Baltimore. British troops threatened New Orleans but were driven off in January 1815 by Andrew Jackson.

Outcome: In the Treaty of Ghent (signed December 24, 1814), both sides agreed to boundaries set up before the war. Britain agreed to end impressment of American seamen and give up British forts south of the Great Lakes. The treaty also settled disputes about fishing rights and commercial relations.

During the war, British troops captured Washington, D.C., and burned the Capitol and the Executive Mansion. In 1814, however, they were defeated when they attacked Baltimore, and U.S. troops turned back an invasion from Canada through New York State. The most memorable battle of the war was fought in January 1815, after the peace treaty had been signed but before news of the treaty had arrived from Europe. A force commanded by General Andrew Jackson defeated a British attack outside New Orleans. Jackson became a national hero and was later elected president. He would have an important role in the life of Martin Van Buren.

The Bucktails

During the war, Van Buren began another battle in New York, this one against DeWitt

Clinton. Clinton was a longtime mayor of New York City and became lieutenant governor of New York State in 1811. Clinton was a Democratic-Republican, but in 1812, he received the Federalist nomination for U.S. president. Federalists were against the war and believed that Clinton would end it if elected president. He lost the election to Democratic-Republican president James Madison. In New York, Clinton was the main sponsor of a plan to build the 300-mile (480 km) Erie Canal across the state to connect the Hudson River to Lake Erie.

Van Buren believed that Clinton was unfaithful to the Democratic-Republican party when he opposed the war and when he ran against a Democratic-Republican president. Van Buren helped organize an anti-Clinton group within the party called the Bucktails. They gained control of the party in New York and in 1815, they arranged to appoint Van Buren *attorney general* of New York. An attorney general is the official in a state or nation responsible for enforcing the laws. He held this position while continuing to serve as state senator. With two important positions and a strong political organization, Van Buren was one of the most powerful politicians in the state.

In 1816, Van Buren was faced with a difficult decision. His opponent DeWitt Clinton had gathered wide support for building the Erie Canal. Now a bill supporting the canal was introduced in the state senate. The canal would require large amounts of money from the federal government. As a Democratic-

DeWitt Clinton and Van Buren were political enemies. Clinton was a longtime mayor of New York City and the main promoter of the Erie Canal. When he later served as governor, he removed Van Buren from state office.

Republican, Van Buren believed the federal government should not pay for such improvements. On the other hand, the Erie Canal could make a huge difference to the state's economy. It would bring thousands of jobs and would one day make New York the most important trading state in the nation. Most New Yorkers wanted the canal built. In the end, Van Buren supported the bill and persuaded other senators to vote for it. The bill passed, and construction soon began.

The biggest winner in the Erie Canal debate was DeWitt Clinton. His support for the canal increased his popularity, and he became governor of New York in 1817. This was bad news for Van Buren and the Bucktails. In 1819, Governor Clinton removed Van Buren from his job as attorney general.

During these years, Van Buren suffered losses to his family. In 1817 and 1818, his father and mother died. Then in early 1819, his wife Hannah died of tuberculosis. Van Buren was grief-stricken over the loss of his wife. In addition, he had to arrange for the care of his four young sons by family members in Kinderhook. In a few short years, three of the people Van Buren loved most in the world were gone.

Even as he grieved, Van Buren poured his energies into politics. Working with party members from around the state, he helped build a powerful political organization, using *patronage* to gain loyal supporters. Party members who held office in state or local government had many jobs to offer. They gave these jobs only to men who would contribute money and time to the party and vote for the party's candidates at every election. Party leaders could also reward loyal members with nominations to local and state elective offices.

Van Buren arranged for a party member to be appointed to the canal commission, which managed the huge job of building the Erie Canal. Through his appointee, Van Buren arranged for loyal Bucktails to get jobs on the project. In return, the workers donated time and money to Bucktail campaigns and voted for Bucktail candidates.

By the end of his state senate term in 1820, Van Buren was the dominant man in New York State government. His organization was so well put together that today we call it a *political machine.* New Yorkers began calling Van Buren's organization the "Albany Regency" because he seemed to rule almost as a king. Even Governor DeWitt Clinton could not pass legislation without the support of Van Buren's group.

Opponents of the Albany Regency believed that it put too much power in the hands of a few men and that it did not represent the will of the people. They nicknamed Van Buren the "Red Fox of Kinderhook" because of the sly way he made political deals, and "the Little Magician" for the way he could always find enough votes in the legislature to pass bills he favored. Van Buren soon got used to these nicknames. He once said that if he was even a tenth as skillful as his enemies claimed, he would have defeated them all long ago.

Chapter 3

Senator Van Buren ────────────

In 1820, Van Buren campaigned for a seat in the United States Senate.
In those days, U.S. senators were elected by the state legislature, not by
a popular election. Van Buren's political machine gathered the needed
votes in the legislature, and in February 1821, Van Buren was elected.

Before the U.S. Senate met, Van Buren attended a convention
in New York to amend the state constitution. He urged the convention
to extend the right to vote to more citizens. Many counties restricted
voting to men who owned a certain amount of property. These rules
disqualified thousands of recent immigrants and tenant farmers (who
rented their land). Van Buren believed that property qualifications for
voting should be lowered or ended. He argued that his beliefs were
right in principle. His opponents worried that he only wanted more
voters to enlist in his political machine.

Finally, Van Buren packed up and moved to Washington, leaving his young sons with family in Kinderhook. This opened a new chapter in his political life. Could the powerful leader of New York State politics succeed in Washington? And could he keep control of the state machine in New York from a distance?

One of the first issues he encountered in the U.S. Senate was slavery. When the United States acquired the Territory of Florida from Spain in 1819, the Senate debated how this new territory should be organized. Should slavery be allowed there? Southern senators assumed it would be allowed, since slavery was allowed in southern states. Northerners disagreed. An increasing number of northerners believed that slavery was wrong and that it should not be allowed in any new territory or state.

Van Buren had to think carefully about the issue. Most of the voters in New York would oppose slavery. Yet he had grown up with slaves in his own house. Later he even owned a slave named Tom. When Tom ran away, Van Buren did not try very hard to get him back. Van Buren proposed that Florida residents should be allowed to keep the slaves they owned, but that no new slaves should be allowed into the territory. This balanced view solved Van Buren's problem, but received little support from other senators. Northerners thought it was too easy on slave owners and southerners thought it was too harsh.

The Election of 1824

Soon Van Buren was embroiled in the presidential election of 1824. President James Monroe was retiring after serving two terms in office. The Federalist party was no longer powerful enough to elect a president. The big question was which Democratic-Republican should be the next president.

The senators favored W. H. Crawford, a former senator from Georgia who was serving as Monroe's secretary of the treasury. Van Buren used his organizational skills to set up Crawford's campaign. Even after Crawford became seriously ill, Van Buren persuaded the congressional caucus to support him for president. Other strong candidates were nominated by states and regions. Tennessee nominated war hero Andrew Jackson, and Kentucky nominated Henry Clay, the longtime Speaker of the House of Representatives. New England states stood behind John Quincy Adams, Monroe's secretary of state.

Van Buren's candidate, Crawford, carried some southern states but finished only third. Andrew Jackson finished first, gaining the most popular votes and the most votes in the electoral college. Because Jackson did not win a majority in the electoral college (half of the votes plus one), the election was decided by the House of Representatives. The House elected Adams, the second-place finisher, deeply angering supporters of Jackson. Van Buren resolved that in the next election he would back a winning candidate.

When Van Buren arrived in Washington in 1821 as a senator from New York, James Monroe (above) was president. In the 1824 presidential election, Van Buren backed Senator Crawford of Georgia, but John Quincy Adams (opposite page) was finally elected.

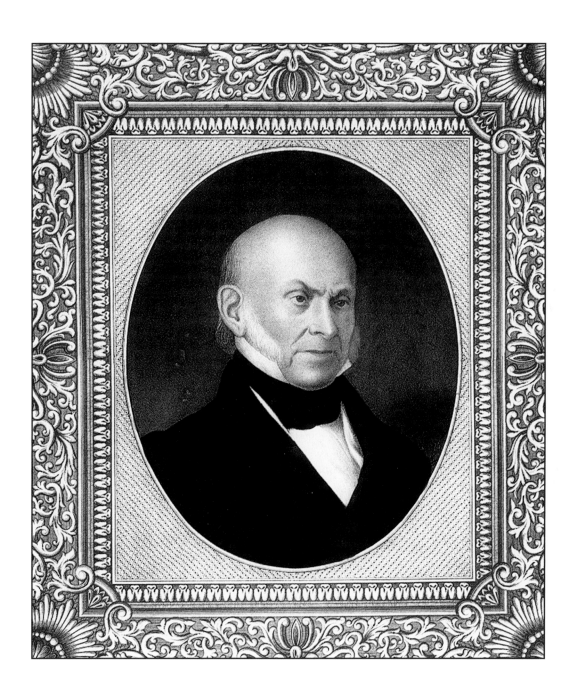

Leaving the Senate

The supporters of Jackson began campaigning to win the presidency in 1828 soon after they lost to Adams in 1825. Jackson was a rough-and-tumble westerner and had been the first major presidential candidate representing a state west of the Appalachian Mountains. Yet his political views were appealing to Van Buren. Both men were traditional Democratic-Republicans, favoring a limited federal government and leaving many government powers to state and local officials. In contrast, President Adams and Henry Clay favored a stronger federal government, and they came to be known as National Republicans.

Finally, Van Buren threw his support behind Andrew Jackson. He became an important leader in Jackson's campaign, introducing methods of organizing that worked so well for him in New York. In the Senate, he worked with others to frustrate the plans and programs of President Adams. Toward the end of Adams's term, Congress passed a tariff bill that it knew would make the president unpopular—in the South if he signed it, and in the North if he refused to sign it.

Meanwhile, back in New York, DeWitt Clinton, who was serving another term as governor, died in office. Van Buren knew that New York was an important state for Jackson to win in the presidential election, and he decided to return home and run for governor. That way he could manage two campaigns—Jackson's and his own—at the same time. He resigned from the Senate and returned to Albany.

Van Buren succeeded in both campaigns. Even though New York had supported Adams for president four years earlier, this time Andrew Jackson won the state. At the same time, Van Buren was elected governor, taking office on January 1, 1829.

Andrew Jackson took office as president on March 4, 1829. At his inaugural reception at the White House, Jackson refused to invite only political leaders. Instead, he invited all of his supporters, calling it a "people's party." Thousands of visitors trooped through the White House, breaking furniture, spilling food and drink, and almost crushing the new president.

Soon after the inauguration, Jackson offered to appoint Van Buren *secretary of state*—the chief manager of the country's foreign affairs and a member of the president's *cabinet*, or group of advisers. Van Buren did not have much background in foreign affairs, but he knew that becoming secretary of state could be a stepping-stone to the presidency. Van Buren resigned as governor to become secretary of state. He had served as governor barely three months.

This print shows the large crowd outside the White House on Jackson's inauguration day in 1829. The artist called it "All Creation Visits the White House."

Andrew Jackson

Andrew Jackson was born in North Carolina in 1767, and he fought in the Revolutionary War when he was only 13 years old. Before the war was over, his mother and two brothers had died, leaving him an orphan. As a teenager, he learned to fight and gamble and stay out late, but he was also a very quick learner. Before he was 20, he passed exams to become a lawyer. Soon afterward, he moved west to Nashville, a wilderness town in present-day Tennessee.

In Nashville, Jackson practiced law, served as a judge, and built a prosperous estate. He found his true calling as a military commander after he was 45 years old. Early in the War of 1812, he gained the nickname "Old Hickory" because of the

In 1828, Andrew Jackson was elected president with strong support from Martin Van Buren, who helped carry New York State for the popular war hero.

tough discipline he used with the Tennessee militia. He became a national hero as commander of the American force that defeated the British at New Orleans in 1815. Later, in 1817, he pursued the Seminole Indians into Florida, where he captured two Spanish forts without government permission. He was nearly censured by Congress, but soon afterward, Spain sold Florida to the United States.

Jackson's straight talk and his suspicion of eastern politicians made him a larger-than-life hero to millions of ordinary citizens. Many of them were voting for the first time in 1828 or 1832, and their votes helped elect "Old Hickory" by huge margins.

☆☆☆

Squabbles in the Cabinet

Jackson's vice president was John C. Calhoun, a Democratic-Republican from South Carolina who also favored limited government and preserving powers for the states. Many people assumed that Calhoun would follow Jackson as president. During Jackson's first term, however, he and Calhoun had several disagreements.

Their first disagreement was about states' rights. Calhoun was upset that northern states wanted to pass high *tariffs* (taxes on goods imported from other countries) that were unpopular in South Carolina. He also worried that northern states might seek to limit slavery. He suggested that a state has the right to *nullify* (refuse to obey) a federal law it believes is unconstitutional and might even have the right to *secede* (withdraw from the United States). Jackson believed that the federal government's powers should be limited, but he also believed that no state had the right to overturn a federal law. In 1830, he proposed a toast at a Democratic-Republican dinner. Looking straight at Calhoun, he raised his glass and said, "To the Union: it must be preserved."

A second disagreement brought an end to Calhoun's hopes to follow Jackson as president. Jackson had one close friend in his cabinet, Secretary of War John Eaton. When Eaton married a young widow named Margaret (Peggy) O'Neill, rumors spread that she was immoral. Vice President Calhoun's wife and other cabinet wives refused to attend any reception to which Peggy Eaton was invited. The attempts to embarrass Peggy Eaton and her husband infuriated President Jackson. He stopped meeting with his cabinet and relied instead on a group of personal advisers known in the newspapers as his "kitchen cabinet."

Van Buren stood up for Peggy and John Eaton, attending receptions and parties with them and always treating Peggy courteously. As the dispute became more and more bitter, Van Buren formed a plan that would

When wives of cabinet members objected to Peggy Eaton, wife of the secretary of war, Jackson and Van Buren came to her defense. The quarrel became so ugly that nearly all cabinet members resigned (including Van Buren).

force the other cabinet members to resign. First, he resigned as secretary of state to protest their treatment of Peggy Eaton. Then President Jackson requested the resignations of all the other cabinet members so that he could reorganize. They gave him written resignations, but they were shocked when he accepted them. Jackson then selected new cabinet members who agreed with him on national policies and would make no objections to Peggy Eaton. Calhoun and his friends in the cabinet were furious.

Vice President John C. Calhoun was angry when Jackson and Van Buren forced other cabinet members to resign. He got his revenge on Van Buren by casting the deciding "no" vote in the Senate against Van Buren's appointment as minister to Great Britain.

Jackson appointed Van Buren *minister* (or ambassador) to Great Britain. Van Buren sailed to England to take up his new duties. He did not stay long, however. His appointment had to be approved by the Senate. Calhoun persuaded his supporters to vote "no," and the vote was tied. This allowed Vice President Calhoun himself to cast the deciding vote. Believing that Van Buren had plotted to get rid of the cabinet, Calhoun voted "no." Van Buren's appointment was turned down, so he had to come home. Soon afterward, Calhoun resigned as vice president and was appointed to the Senate from South Carolina.

Van Buren sailed for home without a position in the government and without any job at all. Still, he had defeated Calhoun, and he remained one of President Jackson's main supporters.

Chapter 4

The Democratic Party

Van Buren arrived in the United States in time for the presidential election in 1832. President Jackson was running for reelection. Van Buren and other Jackson supporters reorganized and decided to run under a new name—the Democratic Party. The new party held its first national convention to nominate its candidates. Jackson was at the height of his popularity, and the delegates to the convention nominated him on the first ballot. With Jackson's support, Van Buren was nominated to run for vice president, winning the required two-thirds of the vote.

Candidates in 1832 did not campaign for themselves, making speeches and appearing at rallies. Jackson and Van Buren worked behind the scenes, while their supporters gave the speeches. The Democrats presented themselves as the party of common people, and they opposed special privileges for the rich. One important campaign issue was the Bank of the United States. This bank was chartered by the government, but it was controlled by private bankers. During his first term, Jackson had vetoed a bill chartering the bank in the future, but its present charter was still good until 1836.

Opponents of Jackson were weak and disorganized. The National Republicans nominated Henry Clay of Kentucky to run against him. Many

Jackson made many enemies in his first term, but was heavily favored to win reelection in 1832. In this cartoon, he is playing brag, a version of poker, with his opponents. He holds three aces — a winning hand.

important businessmen supported the National Republicans, but they did not have enough votes to overcome Jackson. Jackson was reelected easily, winning 219 electoral votes to only 49 for Clay and 18 for other candidates.

On March 4, 1833, Jackson began his second term as president. Van Buren took office as the first vice president elected by the new Democratic party. A few weeks after the election, Jackson turned 66 years old. Although he continued to be a strong leader, he was not healthy, suffering from several old injuries and a series of fevers. Van Buren was younger, at 50 years old, and Jackson relied on him to carry out his policies. The two men were very different in background and appearance, but they had learned to work smoothly together.

Still, Van Buren was not the policy-maker during his vice presidency. Jackson made the policy, and Van Buren's main job was to make sure it was carried out. Van Buren believed in political loyalty, even when he didn't completely agree with a policy. In some of the most difficult issues, he had his doubts, but he continued to support Jackson and the Democratic Party.

Bank Scandal

The main battle during Van Buren's term as vice president was about the Bank of the United States. The small farmers and merchants who helped reelect Jackson believed that the bank was organized to benefit rich bankers and discriminated against the common people. The funds of the federal government were deposited in the bank, giving it large amounts to lend to favored customers. It controlled the supply of paper money, and loaned money to smaller local banks. Bank policies could increase interest rates for small borrowers, making it difficult to get loans to buy land. Jackson's political advisers wanted to weaken the bank or even drive it out of business.

Jackson decided that the best way to weaken the Bank of the United States was to remove all federal money deposited in it. The plan was popular among Democrats, and was supported by many state and local bankers, who hoped that some of the federal money would be deposited in their banks. Jackson went ahead with his plan, but he soon ran into trouble.

The main problem was choosing which other banks the government would put its money into. Van Buren had doubts about the plan, and he tried not to be involved in choosing new banks for government funds. Other Jackson supporters chose the banks and began to deposit federal money. With more resources, the state and local banks began to issue more and more paper currency. At first this made it easier to borrow money and repay loans, but it also caused inflation—the prices of goods increased and a dollar bought less and less. Soon the banks with new federal money were called "pet" banks by Jackson's critics. They accused him of weakening the Bank of the United States to help friends who owned other banks.

Jackson's battle against the Bank of the United States. In this unfriendly cartoon, the bank is a nightmare dragon which is about to devour him. One of his advisers tries to drag him away by his suspenders.

By 1836, Jackson was forced to issue a new rule to slow down inflation. He announced that any money owed to the federal government had to be paid in gold or silver—not in paper money. This new regulation began a "panic." Local banks didn't have enough gold or silver to pay their debts to the Bank of the United States. They asked their borrowers to pay in gold or silver. Paper money became nearly useless. Businesses failed and farmers could not pay for their land. Banks failed, businesses went bankrupt, and soon many people were unemployed. The worst of the economic distress occurred just as Jackson was retiring from the presidency, leaving the problem to Martin Van Buren.

Indian Affairs

Jackson was famous as an Indian fighter who took a hard line against Native Americans. He believed that they should learn to live as their white neighbors lived or they should be moved to uninhabited regions in the west. In 1830, Jackson strongly supported the Indian Removal Act. It allowed the president to remove Native Americans from land inside state borders to new territories in the unsettled western frontier.

In the 1830s, gold was discovered on Cherokee land in Georgia, and white prospectors rushed to the scene. Cherokee leaders refused to give up their land, but in 1835, government commissioners got a few minor Cherokee leaders to sign a treaty surrendering all their land east of the Mississippi River. The main Cherokee leaders, who did not sign the treaty, sued the state of Georgia, and the case was finally decided by the U.S. Supreme Court. It ruled that the treaty was not legal. However, Georgia officials refused to accept the Supreme Court's decision, and President Jackson did not enforce it. So the Cherokee lost their lands anyway. Within a few years, they would be forced to leave Georgia.

Texas

In 1833, when Van Buren became vice president, about 30,000 Americans had moved to Texas, which was then a territory of Mexico. Mexico, governed by Antonio López de Santa Anna, treated the new Texans harshly, allowing them little self-government. In 1836, Texas declared its independence from Mexico and became the Republic of Texas.

Santa Anna himself led troops into Texas. He surrounded a small group of freedom fighters at the Alamo, a fortress in current-day San Antonio. The Texas patriots refused to surrender and fought until the last man was killed. Soon afterward, however, the Texans defeated Santa Anna at San Jacinto. He did not try to recapture Texas, but he refused to recognize its independence.

Many supporters of Jackson wanted the United States to *annex* Texas, making it part of the United States. Many others realized that annexing Texas

When a group of Texas independence fighters was besieged and killed at the Alamo in 1836, Texans were even more determined to be free of Mexican rule. Six weeks later they defeated a Mexican army at San Jacinto and declared their independence.

could cause serious problems. As a former secretary of state, Van Buren knew that claiming Texas could lead to war with Mexico. He also knew that Texas would get involved in the growing debate about slavery. Leaders of Texas favored slavery and would want to be admitted as a slave territory. Northerners, more and more opposed to slavery, would be certain to oppose this. The Texas question would play an important role in Van Buren's future.

Election of 1836

As President Jackson's term drew to a close, he made it clear that he intended Martin Van Buren to become the next president. He and Van Buren began planning the campaign for the 1836 election. The Democratic party unanimously nominated Van Buren for president.

Van Buren was very different from Andrew Jackson. Where Jackson had strong opinions and seemed always to be decisive, Van Buren sometimes seemed to straddle an issue, not taking a definite stand on one side or the other. Although some of his opponents blamed him for this, the issues he faced were very difficult. The issue of slavery, for example, threatened to break the United States in two. Some northerners campaigned for an immediate end to slavery, while some southerners were ready to take their states out of the Union if slavery was limited further. Needing votes from both the North and the South, Van Buren issued a carefully worded statement. He said he believed Congress, the nation's lawmaking body, had the power to abolish slavery in Washington, D.C. But then he said he did not want nationwide *abolition*, getting rid of slavery completely. He promised southerners he would protect slavery in the slave states.

Opponents of Andrew Jackson formed a new political party called the Whigs in 1834 and ran their first presidential candidates against Van Buren in 1836. The Whigs were a major political party in Great Britain that wanted to limit the powers of the monarchy. The Whigs in the United States portrayed Andrew Jackson as "King Andrew the First," complaining that he had gained as much power as a king. The Whigs disagreed about many issues, but they were united in opposing Jackson and Martin Van Buren. They could not agree on a single candidate to run for president, so they ran several candidates in different regions of the country. They hoped that the Whig candidates together could win enough electoral votes to deny Van Buren the presidency.

Andrew Jackson was still the most popular leader in the United States, however. Voters believed that Van Buren would carry on Jackson's policies, continuing to defend common people against the rich and powerful. Van Buren won a few more votes than all of his opponents put together. In the electoral college,

In 1836, the new Whig party ran against Andrew Jackson (who was retiring) and against candidate Van Buren. The Whigs portrayed Jackson as King Andrew the First, who is trampling the Constitution and the Bank of the United States under his feet.

he gained 170 votes, while four other candidates (including three Whigs) won only 124. The most popular Whig was former general William Henry Harrison, who won 74 electoral votes. Van Buren and Harrison would meet again in the next election.

Chapter 5

Eighth President of the United States

A Family White House

Martin Van Buren's term as president began on March 4, 1837. At the inauguration ceremony, he delivered his first address to the nation and was sworn into office. He rode to the ceremony in grand style, carried in a coach made of wood from the famous battleship USS *Constitution* ("Old Ironsides"). Andrew Jackson, though ill, rode beside him.

In his inauguration speech, Van Buren spoke proudly of the United States, its accomplishments since the Revolution, and its good standing in the world. He said that the American republic was one of a kind. With satisfaction he said, "In all the attributes of a great, happy, and flourishing people we stand without a parallel in the world."

A portrait of Martin Van Buren as president.

In truth, the country was not entirely happy. A huge financial panic, or recession, was just beginning. In addition, arguments over states' rights and slavery were beginning to divide the North from the South. Van Buren urged the states to remember that the nation was founded on the principle of *compromise*. The states must be willing to give in on some issues so that the Union as a whole could remain strong.

Normally the vice president would be sworn in on the inauguration day as well. But at that time, the president and vice president were elected separately. That year, none of the four candidates for vice president won a majority

Richard Mentor Johnson

Van Buren's vice president, Richard Mentor Johnson (1780–1850), was a longtime congressman and senator from Kentucky. During the War of 1812, he organized a group of Kentucky riflemen. In the Battle of the Thames River, Johnson and his force fought with great bravery under General William Henry Harrison—Van Buren's Whig opponent in the presidential elections of 1836 and 1840. Johnson was wounded in action.

Johnson missed the inauguration because he had not won a majority of electoral votes for vice president, and he was awaiting a vote by the Senate, as provided in the Constitution. Johnson is the only vice president in history to be chosen by Congress.

☆ ☆ ☆

of electoral votes. The Senate had to decide who would be the vice president, and they later selected Richard Mentor Johnson in a vote of 33 to 16.

All four of Van Buren's sons were in Washington for the inauguration. Two of them, Abraham and Martin Jr., worked for their father in the White House during his presidency. During Andrew Jackson's term, the White House had grown shabby. Van Buren, who enjoyed elegant surroundings, remodeled many of the rooms, ordering new furniture and draperies.

At parties and other functions at the White House, the president's wife traditionally serves as hostess. Van Buren's wife Hannah had been dead for nearly twenty years, and Van Buren had never remarried. For a time, Dolley Madison, the widow of President James Madison, served as White House hostess. Now an elderly woman living in Washington, she was still much admired.

Later, Dolley introduced her young relative Angelica Singleton to the Van Burens. Van Buren's son Abraham fell in love with Angelica, and they were married in 1838. After their honeymoon, they lived in the White House, and Angelica served as the official White House hostess. Although Van Buren grew up in a small town and his family was far from rich, he had developed a taste for elegance. He dressed in fine clothes, and he dined on rich food and costly wine. He enjoyed the theater and later came to appreciate opera. In the White House, he enjoyed entertaining visitors with excellent food and drink.

Since Van Buren was a widower, he asked Dolley Madison (above), widow of former president James Madison, to serve as hostess at White House dinners and receptions. Later, Angelica Singleton Van Buren (opposite page), the beautiful wife of Van Buren's son, served as hostess.

Panic of 1837

Just as President Van Buren took office, the country was facing a serious financial catastrophe. In May 1837, banks across the country failed. Businesses shut down. Thousands of workers lost their jobs, and people lost their farms and homes when they could not pay their mortgages. In some cities there were riots over rising food prices. The United States was in a *depression.*

Americans were frightened and desperate. Politicians wanted President Van Buren to do something to make things better for their constituents. Businessmen wanted the government to do something to restore confidence. Van Buren had always been a problem-solver. Even in difficult circumstances, he usually could find a solution. Now, however, he was in a harsh spotlight. The entire nation was looking at him and waiting for a miracle.

After the failure of major banks in May, Van Buren called a special session of Congress to consider action, but he set the date of the session in September, nearly four months later. He hoped to work out a solution in the months before Congress met. In September, he proposed that the government set up a new and independent treasury to manage the government's money in a way that was best for the whole country. All federal money would be withdrawn from state banks and placed in this treasury.

The Panic of 1837 cast a deep shadow on Van Buren's presidency. In this cartoon, the fat banker stands in the door to the bank, while ordinary people seem to despair. Signs advertise foreclosed farms for sale and offer work building prisons (for people who can't pay their debts) at the rate of 12.5 cents per day.

Van Buren's proposal met an unpleasant response. Politicians did not like the idea of an independent treasury, calling it "cold and heartless." They believed that poor people would be hurt most by Van Buren's system, which was based on gold and silver, not on paper money. Supporters of local and state banks also opposed the plan. They did not want federal money removed from their local banks.

The bill Van Buren supported passed two different times in the Senate, but both times, it was defeated in the House of Representatives, the second time by a

What Caused the Panic of 1837?

Like other panics and depressions, the Panic of 1837 had several causes, and people could not agree on which was the most important. President Jackson's withdrawal of federal money from the Bank of the United States allowed other banks more freedom to lend money. Much of it went to speculators, who bought huge tracts of land in the west, hoping to sell it for more than they paid. When the land lost value, the speculators couldn't repay the money they borrowed.

Just before Jackson left office, he tried to fix the problem. By requiring that land bought from the government had to be paid for with gold or silver, he put further strain on the banks. When people rushed to exchange their paper money for gold and silver, the banks did not have enough precious metal to go around, and the value of paper money fell. To make matters worse, troubled banks in England demanded repayment of loans they had made to American banks.

Like presidents during other depressions, Van Buren found that there was not much he could do to end the hard times.

☆ ★ ☆

The *Amistad* Mutiny

In 1839, a group of African captives on the *Amistad*, a Spanish ship bringing slaves to Cuba, revolted and took over the ship. The slaves ordered the crew to sail back to Africa, but the crew sailed north instead, landing on the shore of Connecticut, where the *Amistad* was seized by the U.S. Navy. The U.S. government had to decide whether to send the captives to Cuba as slaves or back to their home in Africa. A federal court would make the decision.

In court, the federal prosecutor claimed the captives were slaves. As property, they should be returned to the Spanish in Cuba, where slavery was legal. But defenders of the Africans, including former president John Quincy Adams, made strong arguments. Even though slavery was legal in Cuba, they said, the bringing of slaves from Africa was illegal. The captives were kidnap victims who had the right to escape.

President Van Buren was certain the Africans would be sent to Cuba and he ordered a ship to stand by to provide transportation. With this action, he hoped to win proslavery votes in the next election. But the Supreme Court ruled in favor of the captives, who were later returned to Africa.

A mutiny on the slave ship *Amistad* caused public disputes about slavery. Kidnapped Africans took over the ship and killed the captain. They were eventually freed and returned to their homes in Africa.

vote of 120 to 106. The panic continued and no independent treasury could be established, but Van Buren and his supporters continued to fight for the idea. In 1840, they came to agreement with Congress and passed the Independent Treasury Act. It remains one of the outstanding achievements of Van Buren's years in the White House.

The Texas Question and the Trail of Tears ———

The new Republic of Texas hoped that it would soon be annexed by the United States. Southern politicians supported the annexation, seeing that Texas could extend the territories where slavery was permitted. Northern politicians did not want another slave state.

Van Buren had already opposed annexing Texas, since the action would almost certainly bring on war with Mexico. In addition, he wanted to avoid angering proslavery or antislavery groups in the United States. He had supported the right of southern states to practice slavery, and some people expected him to approve the annexation. Van Buren did not want to anger the northern states, either, and he knew that adding a slave territory would raise loud objections in the North. He refused to annex Texas, leaving the issue to later presidents.

Van Buren could not avoid problems with Native Americans. The Second Seminole War began in the Florida Territory even before he was elected, and continued after he left the White House. White settlers wanted the Seminole removed west of the Mississippi River so they could settle the land. Led by Chief Osceola, the Seminoles fought back with great determination. Historians estimate that up to 2,000 U.S. soldiers were killed, and that the U.S. government spent between $40 million and $60 million on the war. After Van Buren's presidency, the Seminole were defeated and forced to move west, but a Third Seminole War was fought in the 1850s to track down those who still lived in Florida.

The long dispute with the Cherokee in Georgia ended during Van Buren's presidency. Under the Indian Removal Act, the Cherokees were required to leave their lands during the fall and winter of 1838–1839. General Winfield Scott, commanding 7,000 U.S. troops, first forced the Cherokees from their homes into camps. Local citizens moved in to plunder and destroy deserted Cherokee homes. Meanwhile, U.S. forces gathered Cherokees in groups of about a thousand and forcibly escorted them to reservations in present-day Oklahoma. This long forced march came to be known as the Trail of Tears. Troops had failed to supply enough food for the travelers. Bitter winter weather caused further suffering. About 4,000 Cherokees died on the trail, many because soldiers would not let the ill and weak stop to rest. The Trail of Tears was a low point in the nation's dealings with Native Americans.

Border with Canada ————————————————

During his first year in office, Van Buren had more than just the depression to deal with. In Canada, near Toronto, a group formed to throw off British rule in Canada. They raised a small army and occupied Navy Island, in the Niagara River, part of the border between Canada and the United States. U.S. citizens who were sympathetic to their cause joined the army. The U.S. steamship *Caroline* carried supplies to Navy Island. In December 1837, troops loyal to Britain seized the *Caroline* in U.S. waters and killed many aboard, including Americans. They set the ship afire and let it drift downstream until it crashed over the Niagara Falls.

Many in the United States wanted to declare war on Britain for this warlike act. Van Buren recognized that the attack on the *Caroline* was an aggressive act, but he also knew that Americans who supported the uprising in Canada had been in the wrong. His administration had taken no position for or against the uprising, holding to his lifelong belief that the United States should remain neutral in the affairs of other countries.

Van Buren sent U.S. troops to occupy the region near the Canadian border where trouble was brewing—not to help the Canadian rebels, but to restrain Americans who supported them. At the same time, he declared the United States

Canadians loyal to Britain set fire to the American ship *Caroline* in the Niagara River after it brought supplies to Canadian rebels seeking independence from Britain. The ship drifted downstream and over the Niagara Falls. Some Americans wanted war against Britain, but Van Buren solved the crisis peacefully.

The States During the Presidency of Martin Van Buren

STATES WHEN PRESIDENT TOOK OFFICE

neutral in the Canada-Britain conflict. He successfully avoided another war with Britain.

In early 1839, Van Buren was again faced with skirmishes on the U.S.-Canadian border in the so-called Aroostook War. The border between Maine and Canada had never been clearly defined. Both countries claimed some 12,000 acres (4,900 hectares) along the Aroostook River. Rufus McIntire, an American, tried to remove Canadians from the land, and the Canadian militia arrested him. No blood was shed in the incident. Van Buren acted once again to preserve peace. He ordered American troops to the area and sent General Winfield Scott to arrange a truce. The dispute was finally settled by the Webster-Ashburton Treaty in 1842, after Van Buren left office.

During the difficult years of 1837–1841, Martin Van Buren led the country through an economic depression, bloody military actions against Native Americans, and threats of war with Britain. He was not responsible for many of these problems, which had begun before he took office, and he had only limited powers to solve them. Even so, many Americans blamed him for difficult times and came to believe that there should be a change in the coming election.

Van Buren must have felt discouraged about the state of the nation, but he behaved with his customary grace and good humor. His handling of a brief crisis in the White House illustrates his ability to remain calm when others panicked.

One evening when he was hosting a dinner, a fire broke out in the kitchen. A kitchen worker slipped up to the president at the dinner table. "The house is on fire!" he exclaimed. Van Buren responded calmly. He got up, went to the kitchen, and helped put out the fire. When the fire was out, one of the dinner guests, Van Buren's old rival Henry Clay, said, "I am doing all I can to get you out of this house; but believe me, I do not want to burn you out."

Chapter 6

Election Defeat

Van Buren had been elected to carry on the policies of President Andrew Jackson. Now, four years later, Jackson was in retirement in Tennessee, and for many citizens times were very hard. Van Buren's popularity seemed to disappear, and his hopes for reelection seemed very dim.

The Whigs, who had organized to oppose Andrew Jackson's policies, saw that they had an opportunity to elect the first Whig president. Their leaders included such powerful congressional leaders as Henry Clay and Daniel Webster, but both men had as many enemies as they had friends. At the Whig convention, the delegates nominated a war hero from the western frontier, William Henry Harrison, as their presidential candidate. In the campaign, Harrison was often known as

"Tippecanoe" after his famous victory over the Shawnee on the Tippecanoe River in the Indiana Territory in 1811. He was portrayed as a simple westerner who lived in a log cabin, not in a mansion, and who drank inexpensive hard cider, not expensive wines.

The Whig campaign against Van Buren attacked his expensive tastes in clothing, food, and wine, and called him King Martin I. They also pointed out that Van Buren had been unable to end the hard times which were causing so much suffering. "Van, Van, is a used up man!" they chanted. They presented Harrison as the new champion of ordinary working people.

Van Buren Is OK

In 1840, newspapers in the northeastern states began using the odd abbreviation "OK" to mean "good" or "excellent." It probably originated from a joke about a poorly trained schoolteacher who marked a test with no wrong answers "OK" to stand for "oll korrect."

Van Buren's campaign picked up the term, saying that their candidate was "OK," and claiming the letters stood for "Old Kinderhook." In this strange way, Van Buren's name is associated with the expression, which is now used worldwide.

☆ ★ ☆

A HARD ROAD TO HOE

Or, the White House Turnpike, macadamized by the North Benders.

Van Buren seemed sure to lose the 1840 election campaign. This cartoon shows his road to the White House obstructed by log cabins and hard cider barrels — the symbols of the Whigs' campaign for Harrison. In the other direction, the road sign shows the way to Kinderhook, where Van Buren would retire when he lost the election.

Most important, the Whigs organized parades and rallies for their candidate throughout the country. Women participated in the campaign by making handicrafts featuring the log cabin and a keg of hard cider. Many parades featured huge balls ten feet (three meters) high that were rolled from town to town and carried the slogan "Keep the Ball Rolling for Harrison."

On election day, Van Buren went down in defeat. William Henry Harrison carried a large majority of the states and received 234 votes in the electoral college to only 60 for Van Buren. Van Buren's days in the White House were over.

Harrison, at 68, was the oldest president to be elected up to that time, but he showed amazing energy as he entered office. On a cold, rainy inauguration

Whig campaigners roll this huge ball in a parade. Writing on the side says, "Fare well dear Van / Not the man / To guide the ship."

day, he gave the longest inauguration address in history—lasting an hour and forty minutes. Then, only a few weeks into his term, he fell ill. He died on April 4, 1841, less than a month after he took office. Vice President John Tyler became president and served out the four-year term.

Van Buren returned to his hometown of Kinderhook, New York. In 1839, he had bought a large estate called Lindenwald from his old friends, the Van Ness family. He paid $14,000 for the house and 200 acres (80 hectares) of land around it, which he turned into a working farm. Over the years he added more acreage to the farm and made modern improvements to the two-story brick home. He added ranges for cooking in the kitchen, and he installed running water and a hot-water heater.

After a lifetime of dedication to public affairs, Van Buren now had time to relax and pursue leisure activities. He enjoyed fishing and visiting old friends, and he took pride in farming his potato and turnip fields. But he could not convince himself to stay in retirement for long.

Slow Good-bye to the Presidency ———————

Early in 1841, the Missouri legislature officially nominated Van Buren as a presidential candidate for the next election, in 1844. That election was nearly four years in the future, but Van Buren began touring the country. He focused

Lindenwald, Van Buren's estate near Kinderhook, where he retired after losing his campaign for reelection in 1840. Today it is a National Historic Site.

on the southern and western states, where he most needed to increase his support.

A key campaign issue was the Texas Question. Should Texas be annexed and made part of the United States? As president, Van Buren had not supported Texas's bid for annexation, and he held to this position. His stand on the Texas Question finally sank his hopes for the Democratic nomination. His old mentor, Andrew Jackson, came to favor the annexation of Texas. When Van Buren would not change his views, Jackson supported James K. Polk. At the Democratic party convention in 1844, Van Buren won a majority of the delegates' votes to become the presidential nominee on the first ballot, but convention rules required that the nominee gain two-thirds of the votes. In later ballots, the candidates favoring annexation threw their support to Polk, and he was nominated. Polk won the election of 1844, and even before he took office, Texas became a territory of the United States.

Even after this second defeat, Van Buren lost none of his fervor for politics. Now he took up a new issue, speaking out more strongly against slavery instead of taking a middle-of-the-road stance as he had done before. The Democratic party in New York State was divided on the issue of slavery. One group, the Hunkers, took a conservative view. It had always existed in the South, they said, and should be allowed to continue. They accused antislavery

Free Soil Party

The Free Soil party was formed in 1848 by Democrats and Whigs who disagreed with their parties' position on slavery. Free Soilers wanted to restrict slavery in new states being added to the Union. At its founding convention in Buffalo, New York, the party nominated Martin Van Buren for president and Charles Francis Adams (son of John Quincy Adams) for vice president.

☆★☆

Democrats of threatening the Union, suggesting that southern states might leave the United States if new restrictions were made on slavery.

Van Buren and his son John helped form a more radical group calling for the government to outlaw slavery in all new states and territories. Their opponents called them the Barnburners, suggesting that they were like the farmer in the story who burned down his barn to get rid of the rats. When the Democratic convention nominated Lewis Cass, a Hunker candidate, the Barnburners walked out.

Later in 1848, the Barnburners joined with the new Free Soil Party to run a third-party candidate for president. The Free Soil Party nominated Van Buren. The Whigs nominated a hero of the Mexican War, Zachary Taylor. Van Buren ran a distant third in the election, but he got more votes in New York State than Lewis Cass. Taylor carried the state for the Whigs and was elected president.

In 1848, Van Buren ran for president on the third-party Free Soil ticket. This cartoon shows his hopeless attempt to bridge the differences between Democrats on the right and Whigs on the left. He is about to fall in the "Salt River," a popular cartoon image for political defeat.

Elder Statesman

After three failed attempts to get reelected as president, Van Buren did not run

again. He retired from active politics, but he never lost interest in political affairs.

As an elder statesman, he was still respected by many, and he was often asked for advice or opinions on political matters. He lent his support to the candidacies of Democrats Franklin Pierce in 1852 and James Buchanan in 1856.

Between his political activities, Van Buren found time to see a little of the world. For two years in the early 1850s, he toured Europe. He was the first ex-president to leave the United States. He visited the Netherlands, the home of his Dutch ancestors. In England he was received by Queen Victoria. Then he lived in Italy for a while. There, he began writing his autobiography. He never finished this work.

The Final Years

When Van Buren returned from Europe in 1855, he studied the rising tensions between the North and the South. After 1857, he was disappointed in President Buchanan's leadership of the country. Still, Van Buren remained a loyal Democrat, and in 1860 he supported the party's candidate, Stephen A. Douglas, against the candidate of the new Republican party, Abraham Lincoln. Lincoln was elected, and before he took office, southern states began seceding from the Union. Soon after Lincoln took office in 1861, the Civil War began. As the North took up arms against the South, Van Buren announced his support for President Lincoln, who pledged to fight to preserve the Union.

Fast Facts

What: A war between the Northern and Southern states of the United States

When: 1861–1865

Who: The North maintained control of the federal government and called itself the Union. The southern states seceded from the Union and formed the Confederate States of America.

Where: Major eastern battles in Virginia, Maryland, and Pennsylvania. Major western battles in Tennessee, Mississippi, and western Georgia. Union troops took control of the Mississippi River and later captured Georgia, dividing the Confederacy.

Why: The Union argued that states had no right to secede from the United States and insisted that the federal government had the right to make laws concerning slavery. The Confederacy argued that states can secede and that choices about slavery should be made by individual states, not the federal government.

Outcome: After victorious campaigns in the west and south, Union armies invaded Virginia, and forced the surrender of the largest remaining Confederate Army at Appomattox, Virginia, in April 1865. The restored Union passed constitutional amendments abolishing slavery and guaranteeing civil rights to citizens regardless of race. It also imposed harsh restrictions on the former Confederate states under a program called Reconstruction.

Van Buren did not live to see the outcome of the Civil War. The elder statesman died at Lindenwald on July 24, 1862. He was seventy-nine years old. His funeral was held at the Dutch Reformed church in Kinderhook, and a procession of 80 carriages escorted his coffin to the nearby cemetery. He was buried beside his wife and parents. The former president's estate, valued at about $225,000, went to his three surviving sons.

Chapter 7

The Crafty Politician —————————

As Martin Van Buren began his presidency, he drew inspiration from the founders of the nation and from previous presidents. In his inauguration address, he said, "I tread in the footsteps of illustrious men." Yet he focused more on the future than the past. He listed the principles on which the country was founded—civil and religious freedoms for citizens, and a willingness among the states to compromise for the greater good. He said that these principles "are destined to confer their benefits on countless generations yet to come, and that America will present to every friend of mankind the cheering proof that a popular government, wisely formed, is wanting [lacking] in no element of endurance or strength."

At his death more than twenty years later, however, Van Buren's legacy was not easy to define. He entered office in the shadow of a national hero, Andrew Jackson, and served during a severe economic depression which he had few powers to end. Opponents found him an easy target, pointing to his early career as a "machine" politician in New York and as a skilled campaign manager for Andrew Jackson and others. Earlier presidents such as Washington, Jefferson, and Jackson came to office as heroes. Van Buren was seen as a skilled and crafty politician, the "Red Fox of Kinderhook."

The Economy

The great challenge of Van Buren's presidency was the economy. Earlier, he had supported Andrew Jackson's campaign to destroy the Bank of the United States and his later effort to steady the economy by requiring government debts to be paid with gold or silver. By the time Van Buren took office, the bank was destroyed, and the gold requirement helped cause a panic. Banks closed, thousands were out of work, and prices were rising.

During the "Panic Session," the special session of Congress in 1837 to discuss the Panic, Van Buren proposed an independent treasury and "separating" federal money from local banks, but Congress rejected the idea. He continued to fight for the plan. Three years later, he was finally successful. On July 4, 1840, Congress passed the Independent Treasury Act. It was a first step toward the system the federal government uses today.

Martin Van Buren about 1848.

Earlier, Van Buren established a plan to ease the pain of economic depression in New York State. During his brief time as governor in 1829, he sponsored the Safety Fund Plan, which required every bank in the state to set up a special safety fund to pay back its investors if it went out of business. Later, other state banks followed the example of New York banks. Much later, during the Great Depression of the 1930s, the federal government set up the Federal Deposit Insurance Corporation (FDIC), which insures the deposits of bank customers.

The American Political System

Van Buren's greatest contribution was his leadership in developing the modern party system in U.S. politics. In New York, he helped create the first powerful political machine, the Albany Regency, which gained broad power in the state by offering jobs and political appointments to citizens who loyally supported the party. Through this organization, Van Buren was a powerful boss in New York long after he was elected to national office and moved to Washington.

In 1828, Van Buren was perhaps the first campaign director of a presidential campaign, using political organization and new campaign techniques to bring Andrew Jackson a landslide victory. During his eight years of service in the Jackson administration, he was the organizer of the modern Democratic Party, which dominated U.S. politics from 1828 to 1860. The party has continued as a major political organization to the present day.

Abolition at Last

Late in his career, Van Buren also contributed to the huge changes that were taking place in American attitudes toward slavery. He grew up in a household that owned slaves and later struggled to find a middle position on slavery that could get him elected in a divided country. After he left the White House, however, his views began to change. In 1846, he came out in support of the Wilmot Proviso, which would prohibit slavery in new territories. In 1848, as leader of the Barnburners, he took a stand with Democrats who opposed extending slavery, and that year he joined with the Free Soil party and ran as the antislavery candidate for president. He lost, but the votes he gained helped defeat Democrat Lewis Cass and elect Whig Zachary Taylor, who was against the admission of slave states to the Union. In his final two years of life, Van Buren used his influence as a former president to support President Abraham Lincoln. In the war against slavery, Van Buren had become an abolitionist.

As an individual, Van Buren inspired warm friendship in some—and snide criticism in others. His friend Washington Irving wrote in 1832, "The more

A photograph of Van Buren in his last years taken by the famous photographer Mathew Brady, set in a gilt (gold-coated) frame.

I see of Mr. V.B., the more I feel confirmed in a strong personal regard for him. He is one of the gentlest and most amiable men I have ever met with."

On the other hand, Davy Crockett, the famous frontiersman and congressman from Tennessee, ridiculed Van Buren. Van Buren, said Crockett in 1835, "is what the English call a dandy. When he enters the senate chamber in the morning, he struts and swaggers like a crow in the gutter. He is laced up in corsets, such as women in town wear, and, if possible, tighter than the best of them. It would be difficult to say, from his personal appearance, whether he was a man or woman, but for his large . . . whiskers."

Above all, Van Buren was the first politician as we understand the word today. He became famous—or infamous, as the case may be—for his skill at being hard to pin down on controversial issues. John Randolph, a political leader from Virginia, once said that Van Buren "rowed to his object with muffled oars." Yet in the end, he was able to toss aside his muffled oars. By changing his position on slavery, the nation's first "political president" showed that even a skilled politician must one day take a stand.

Fast Facts
Martin Van Buren

Birth:	December 5, 1782
Birthplace:	Kinderhook, New York
Parents:	Abraham and Maria Hoes Van Buren
Sisters & Brothers:	1 half sister and 2 half brothers
	1 sister: Derike (1777–1865)
	2 brothers: Lawrence (1786–1868), Abraham (1788–1836)
	(2 other sisters died in infancy)
Education:	Studied law by apprenticeship in Kinderhook and New York City
Occupation:	Lawyer
Marriage:	To Hannah Hoes Van Buren (1783–1819), February 21, 1807
	(Van Buren never remarried after Hannah's death)
Children:	Abraham (1807–1873), John (1810–1866),
	Martin Jr. (1812–1855), Smith (1817–1876)
Political Party:	Democratic-Republican Party; Democratic Party
Government Service:	1808–1813 Surrogate of Columbia County (NY)
	1813–1820 New York State Senator
	1815–1819 Attorney General of New York
	1821–1829 U.S. Senator from New York
	1829 Governor of New York
	1829–1831 U.S. Secretary of State under President Andrew Jackson
	1833–1837 U.S. Vice President under Jackson
	1837–1841 Eighth President of the United States
His Vice President:	Richard Mentor Johnson (1781–1850)
Major Actions as President:	1837 Called special session of Congress to consider the Panic of 1837
	1837 Sent U.S. troops to New York State to keep peace after Canadians burned a U.S. ship in the Niagara River
	1838 Supported action to remove Cherokee from Georgia, leading to the Trail of Tears
	1839 Sent U.S. troops to Maine to avoid war over Maine-Canada border
	1840 Signed the Independent Treasury Act, the first step toward the modern Treasury Department
Firsts:	First born under the United States flag
	First not of British ancestry; first of Dutch ancestry
Death:	July 24, 1862
Age at Death:	79 years
Burial Place:	Kinderhook, New York

Fast Facts Hannah Hoes Van Buren

Birth:	March 8, 1783
Birthplace:	Kinderhook, New York
Parents:	Johannes and Maria Quackenbush Hoes
Sisters & Brothers:	(not known)
Marriage:	To Martin Van Buren, February 21, 1807
Children:	Four sons (*see* Martin Van Buren at left)
Death:	February 5, 1819 (18 years before Van Buren became president)
Age at Death:	35 years
Burial Place:	Kinderhook, New York

Timeline

1782	1787	1797	1803	1807
Treaty of Paris ends the American Revolution, November; Martin Van Buren is born December 5 in Kinderhook, New York	United States Constitution is adopted	Van Buren becomes a lawyer's apprentice	Licensed to practice law	Marries Hannah Hoes on February 21

1821–28	1828	1829	1831	1832
Serves as United States senator	Elected governor of New York	Takes office as governor, January; is appointed secretary of state by President Andrew Jackson, March	Resigns as secretary of state during the Eaton Affair; is nominated U.S. minister to Great Britain; when nomination fails in Senate, Van Buren is recalled	Democratic Party nominates Van Buren for vice president at its first national convention; Jackson and Van Buren are elected

1839	1840	1844	1845	1848
Van Buren sends troops to Maine to avoid bloodshed in the Aroostook War over Maine-Canada border	Van Buren signs Independent Treasury Act, July; runs for president, but is defeated by William Henry Harrison, November	Van Buren campaigns for presidency, but Democratic Party nominates James K. Polk instead; Polk wins the election	U.S. annexes Texas; Van Buren leads the Barnburners, Democrats opposed to extending slavery	The antislavery Free Soil party nominates Van Buren for president; he finishes third and Whig Zachary Taylor is elected

1808–13	1812	1813–20	1815–19	1819
Serves as surrogate of Columbia County (NY)	Becomes leader of New York State Democratic-Republican Party	Serves as New York State senator	Serves as New York attorney general	Van Buren's wife Hannah dies at age 35; Van Buren is removed as attorney general

1833	1834	1836	1837	1838-39
Van Buren takes office as vice president	Whig Party is formed to oppose Jackson and the Democrats	Democratic party nominates Van Buren for president and he is elected; Texas declares independence from Mexico	Van Buren is inaugurated as president March 4; Panic of 1837 begins, May; special session of Congress meets, September	Cherokee are forcibly transported to Indian Territory in the Trail of Tears

1861	1862
American Civil War (1861–1865) begins in April; Van Buren announces his support for President Abraham Lincoln	Van Buren dies, July 24, in Kinderhook, New York

Glossary

abolition: in U.S. history, favoring the immediate end of slavery

annex: to join a piece of land to a nation; in 1845 the United States annexed the Republic of Texas

attorney general: the officer of a state or nation responsible for enforcing the laws

bill: a formal proposal for a new law; in the U.S. government, a bill becomes a law when it has been approved by both houses of Congress and signed by the president.

cabinet: leaders of federal departments who meet to advise the president

compromise: an agreement in which disagreeing groups each give up some of what they want to settle their dispute

Congress: the lawmaking body of the United States; it contains the Senate and the House of Representatives

depression: a period of economic slowdown when businesses fail and many people are out of work

federal: in the United States, having to do with national government, as opposed to state or local governments

minister: a person representing the government of one country in another; an ambassador

nullify: in U.S. history, for a state or local government to declare a federal law unconstitutional and refuse to obey or enforce it

patronage: awards of jobs, contracts, or other benefits by a political organization to people loyal to the organization

political machine: a powerful organization that controls the politics in a city or state

secede: in U.S. history, for a state to declare that it has withdrawn from the United States

secretary of state: the officer in the federal government in charge of relations with other countries

tariff: a tax placed on goods being imported into a country

Union: another name for the United States; during the Civil War, the Union consisted of the states in the North after states in the South seceded

Further Reading

Bredeson, Carmen. *The Battle of the Alamo: The Fight for Texas Territory.* Brookfield, CT: Millbrook Press, 1996.

Ferry, Steven. *Martin Van Buren: Our Eighth President.* Chanhassen, MN: The Child's World, 2002.

Fish, Bruce, and Becky Durost Fish. *The History of the Democratic Party.* Philadelphia: Chelsea House Publishers, 2000.

Gay, Kathlyn, and Martin Gay. *War of 1812.* New York: Twenty-First Century Books, 1995.

Hargrove, Jim. *Martin Van Buren: Eighth President of the United States.* Encyclopedia of Presidents. Chicago: Children's Press, 1987.

Harris, Laurie Lanzen, editor. *Presidents of the United States.* Biography for Beginners. Detroit: Omnigraphics, Favorable Impressions, 1998.

Kent, Deborah. *The Star-Spangled Banner.* Chicago: Children's Press, 1995.

Myers, Walter Dean. *Amistad: A Long Road to Freedom.* New York: Dutton Children's Books, 1998.

Stein, Conrad R. *The Trail of Tears.* Revised edition. Chicago: Children's Press, 1993.

Welsbacher, Anne. *Martin Van Buren.* United States Presidents. Edina, MN: ABDO Publishing, 2001.

MORE ADVANCED READING

Niven, John. *Martin Van Buren: The Romantic Age of American Politics.* New York: Oxford University Press, 1983.

Sibley, Joel H. *Martin Van Buren and the Emergence of American Popular Politics.* New York: Rowman & Littlefield, 2002.

Wilson, Major L. *The Presidency of Martin Van Buren.* Lawrence, KS: University Press of Kansas, 1984.

Places to Visit

★ ★ ★ ★ ★

Martin Van Buren National Historic Site
Lindenwald Residence
1013 Old Post Road
P.O. Box 545
Kinderhook, NY 12106
(518) 758-9689

The home to which Van Buren retired after
his presidency and where he died in 1862.
The house in which he was born is also in
Kinderhook at 46 Hudson Street.

The White House
1600 Pennsylvania Avenue
Washington, D.C. 20500
(202) 456-7041

The Alamo
300 Alamo Plaza
San Antonio, TX 78299
(210) 255-1391

Site of the famous siege of Texas patriots by
a Mexican army in 1836. The Texans fought
to the last man, finally losing the fort to
Mexico. Not long afterward, however,
Texans won a decisive victory over the army
of Mexican general Santa Anna at San
Jacinto. Andrew Jackson recognized Texas
as an independent state in 1837, just before
Van Buren became president.

Online Sites of Interest

★★★★★

★**The American Presidency**

http://gi.grolier.com/presidents/ea/bios/08pvanb.html

A site that provides biographies of Van Buren (and all other presidents) at different reading levels, taken from the encyclopedias published by Scholastic Library Publishing/Grolier.

★**American Presidents**

http://www.americanpresidents.org/

Material originally prepared for public television has been used to create a site offering broad coverage of each president.

★**Internet Public Library: President of the United States (IPL-POTUS)**

http://www.ipl.org/ref/POTUS/mvanburen.html

Offers basic information on Van Buren and is especially useful for its links to other sites of interest.

★**Martin Van Buren's Inaugural Address**

http://gi.grolier.com/presidents/ea/inaugs/1837vanb.html

The address may also be found at

http://www.bartleby.org

★**Martin Van Buren National Historic Site**

http://www.nps.gov/mava/

★**Kinderhook History**

http://www.kinderhookconnection.com/index.htm

★**Aroostook War**

http://homepages.rootsweb.com/~godwin/reference/aroostook.html

★**Seminole of Florida**

http://dhr.dos.state.fl.us/flafacts/seminole.html

★**Trail of Tears**

http://ngeorgia.com/history/nghisttt.html

http://rosecity.net/tears/

Table of Presidents

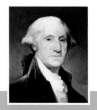   

	1. George Washington	**2. John Adams**	**3. Thomas Jefferson**	**4. James Madison**
Took office	Apr 30 1789	Mar 4 1797	Mar 4 1801	Mar 4 1809
Left office	Mar 3 1797	Mar 3 1801	Mar 3 1809	Mar 3 1817
Birthplace	Westmoreland Co, VA	Braintree, MA	Shadwell, VA	Port Conway, VA
Birth date	Feb 22 1732	Oct 20 1735	Apr 13 1743	Mar 16 1751
Death date	Dec 14 1799	July 4 1826	July 4 1826	June 28 1836

	9. William H. Harrison	**10. John Tyler**	**11. James K. Polk**	**12. Zachary Taylor**
Took office	Mar 4 1841	Apr 6 1841	Mar 4 1845	Mar 5 1849
Left office	**Apr 4 1841•**	Mar 3 1845	Mar 3 1849	**July 9 1850•**
Birthplace	Berkeley, VA	Greenway, VA	Mecklenburg Co, NC	Barboursville, VA
Birth date	Feb 9 1773	Mar 29 1790	Nov 2 1795	Nov 24 1784
Death date	Apr 4 1841	Jan 18 1862	June 15 1849	July 9 1850

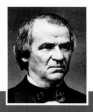  

	17. Andrew Johnson	**18. Ulysses S. Grant**	**19. Rutherford B. Hayes**	**20. James A. Garfield**
Took office	Apr 15 1865	Mar 4 1869	Mar 4 1877	Mar 4 1881
Left office	Mar 3 1869	Mar 3 1877	Mar 3 1881	**Sept 19 1881•**
Birthplace	Raleigh, NC	Point Pleasant, OH	Delaware, OH	Orange, OH
Birth date	Dec 29 1808	Apr 27 1822	Oct 4 1822	Nov 19 1831
Death date	July 31 1875	July 23 1885	Jan 17 1893	Sept 19 1881

5. James Monroe

Mar 4 1817

Mar 3 1825

Westmoreland Co, VA

Apr 28 1758

July 4 1831

6. John Quincy Adams

Mar 4 1825

Mar 3 1829

Braintree, MA

July 11 1767

Feb 23 1848

7. Andrew Jackson

Mar 4 1829

Mar 3 1837

The Waxhaws, SC

Mar 15 1767

June 8 1845

8. Martin Van Buren

Mar 4 1837

Mar 3 1841

Kinderhook, NY

Dec 5 1782

July 24 1862

13. Millard Fillmore

July 9 1850

Mar 3 1853

Locke Township, NY

Jan 7 1800

Mar 8 1874

14. Franklin Pierce

Mar 4 1853

Mar 3 1857

Hillsborough, NH

Nov 23 1804

Oct 8 1869

15. James Buchanan

Mar 4 1857

Mar 3 1861

Cove Gap, PA

Apr 23 1791

June 1 1868

16. Abraham Lincoln

Mar 4 1861

Apr 15 1865•

Hardin Co, KY

Feb 12 1809

Apr 15 1865

21. Chester A. Arthur

Sept 19 1881

Mar 3 1885

Fairfield, VT

Oct 5 1830

Nov 18 1886

22. Grover Cleveland

Mar 4 1885

Mar 3 1889

Caldwell, NJ

Mar 18 1837

June 24 1908

23. Benjamin Harrison

Mar 4 1889

Mar 3 1893

North Bend, OH

Aug 20 1833

Mar 13 1901

24. Grover Cleveland

Mar 4 1893

Mar 3 1897

Caldwell, NJ

Mar 18 1837

June 24 1908

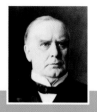

25. William McKinley   **26. Theodore Roosevelt**   **27. William H. Taft**   **28. Woodrow Wilson**

Took office	Mar 4 1897	Sept 14 1901	Mar 4 1909	Mar 4 1913
Left office	**Sept 14 1901•**	Mar 3 1909	Mar 3 1913	Mar 3 1921
Birthplace	Niles, OH	New York, NY	Cincinnati, OH	Staunton, VA
Birth date	Jan 29 1843	Oct 27 1858	Sept 15 1857	Dec 28 1856
Death date	Sept 14 1901	Jan 6 1919	Mar 8 1930	Feb 3 1924

33. Harry S. Truman   **34. Dwight D. Eisenhower**   **35. John F. Kennedy**   **36. Lyndon B. Johnson**

Took office	Apr 12 1945	Jan 20 1953	Jan 20 1961	Nov 22 1963
Left office	Jan 20 1953	Jan 20 1961	**Nov 22 1963•**	Jan 20 1969
Birthplace	Lamar, MO	Denison, TX	Brookline, MA	Johnson City, TX
Birth date	May 8 1884	Oct 14 1890	May 29 1917	Aug 27 1908
Death date	Dec 26 1972	Mar 28 1969	Nov 22 1963	Jan 22 1973

41. George Bush   **42. Bill Clinton**   **43. George W. Bush**

Took office	Jan 20 1989	Jan 20 1993	Jan 20 2001
Left office	Jan 20 1993	Jan 20 2001	—
Birthplace	Milton, MA	Hope, AR	New Haven, CT
Birth date	June 12 1924	Aug 19 1946	July 6 1946
Death date	—	—	—

29. Warren G. Harding	**30. Calvin Coolidge**	**31. Herbert Hoover**	**32. Franklin D. Roosevelt**
Mar 4 1921	Aug 2 1923	Mar 4 1929	Mar 4 1933
Aug 2 1923•	Mar 3 1929	Mar 3 1933	**Apr 12 1945•**
Blooming Grove, OH	Plymouth, VT	West Branch, IA	Hyde Park, NY
Nov 21 1865	July 4 1872	Aug 10 1874	Jan 30 1882
Aug 2 1923	Jan 5 1933	Oct 20 1964	Apr 12 1945

37. Richard M. Nixon	**38. Gerald R. Ford**	**39. Jimmy Carter**	**40. Ronald Reagan**
Jan 20 1969	Aug 9 1974	Jan 20 1977	Jan 20 1981
Aug 9 1974★	Jan 20 1977	Jan 20 1981	Jan 20 1989
Yorba Linda, CA	Omaha, NE	Plains, GA	Tampico, IL
Jan 9 1913	July 14 1913	Oct 1 1924	Feb 11 1911
Apr 22 1994	—	—	—

• Indicates the president died while in office.
★ Richard Nixon resigned before his term expired.

Index

About the Author

Lesli J. Favor finds studying and writing about the lives of others to be much like archeology, but with words. She couldn't resist "excavating" the life and career of The Little Magician, Martin Van Buren. She is the author of *Everything You Need to Know About Growth Spurts and Delayed Growth*, and other books on Francisco Vázquez de Coronado, the Iroquois Confederacy, and Italy. She holds the Ph.D. degree from the University of North Texas. She has taught at North Texas and at Sul Ross State University—Rio Grande College. She lives in Dallas, Texas, with her husband, Steve.